# The Messy Chef's Kitchen

## PARENTAL COOKBOOK

BUILDING RAPPORT
WITH CHILDREN
THROUGH COOKING
TOGETHER

**Traditional Recipes by**

Dr. April A. Jones

# Copyright©

Sankofa Publishing 2024
All rights reserved. Published in the United States by Dr. April A. Jones, a division of Sankofa Achievement Center, Inc. Nashville, Tennessee.

www.thesac.org
Library of Congress Cataloging-Publication Data
Names: Dr. April A. Jones, Author.
Title: The Messy Chef's Kitchen: Parental Cook Book Building Rapport with Children through cooking together
Identifiers ISBN- Print 978-1-7379930-7-0
E-Book 978-1-7379930-8-7

Illustration Dr. April A. Jones

Manufactured in the United States of America

# Dedications

I DEDICATE THIS BOOK TO MY MOTHER AND ALL MOTHERS WHO FIND A WAY OUT OF NO WAY TO FEED AND NURTURE THEIR CHILDREN ON A DAILY BASIS.

MOTHERS ARE THE UNSUNG HEROES OF OUR SOCIETY. THEY WORK TIRELESSLY TO PROVIDE FOR THEIR FAMILIES, OFTEN SACRIFICING THEIR OWN NEEDS AND DESIRES IN THE PROCESS. WHETHER IT'S WAKING UP EARLY TO MAKE BREAKFAST, PACKING LUNCHES, OR STAYING UP LATE TO FINISH LAUNDRY, MOTHERS ARE ALWAYS THERE FOR THEIR CHILDREN. THEY ARE THE ULTIMATE MULTITASKERS, JUGGLING COUNTLESS RESPONSIBILITIES WITH EASE AND GRACE.

DESPITE THE CHALLENGES THEY FACE, MOTHERS CONTINUE TO PERSEVERE, DRIVEN BY THEIR LOVE FOR THEIR CHILDREN. THEY ARE THE ONES WHO TEACH US TO WALK, TALK, AND NAVIGATE THE WORLD AROUND US. THEY ARE OUR FIRST TEACHERS, OUR FIRST FRIENDS, AND OUR FIRST ROLE MODELS.

SO LET US TAKE A MOMENT TO HONOR THE MOTHERS IN OUR LIVES. LET US THANK THEM FOR THEIR UNWAVERING LOVE AND SUPPORT, AND FOR ALL THE SACRIFICES THEY HAVE MADE ON OUR BEHALF. AND LET US REMEMBER THAT THEIR HARD WORK AND DEDICATION HAVE HELPED SHAPE US INTO THE PEOPLE WE ARE TODAY.

# Table of Contents

## 01 - SOUPS & STARTERS
- 01 - TACO SOUP
- 02 - VEGETABLE SOUP
- 03 - SHRIMP SKEWERS
- 04 - MESSY NACHOS
- 05 - CHICKEN SOUP

## 02 - SALADS
- 06 - GLAZED SALMON
- 07 - GRILLED CHICKEN
- 08 - MESSY COBB
- 09 - GREEN SALAD

## 03 - SEAFOOD
- 10 - CAJUN SEAFOOD HOBO POUCHES
- 11 - SAC FRIED FISH SANDWHICH
- 12 - BAKED FISH
- 13 - SEAFOOD BOIL

## 04 - MEAT DISHES
- 14 - TURKEY MEATLOAF
- 15 - STUFFED BELL PEPPERS
- 16 - HOMEMADE DOUBLE BACON CHEESEBURGER
- 17 - CRAZY TACOS
- 18 - SALMON CROQUETTES
- 19 - PINTO BEAN CHILI

## 05 - DESSERTS
- 20 - CANDIED POPCORN
- 21 - WHITE CHOCOLATE PEPPERMINT COVERED PRETZELS
- 22 - MIXED BERRY PARFAIT
- 23 - PEANUT BUTTER CHEESECAKE WITH RASPBERRY JELLY TOPPING

## 06 - PASTA, RICE & GRAINS
- 24 - PASTA WITH SAUSAGE & PEPPERS
- 25 - HOMEMADE TURKEY TETRAZZINI
- 26 - LASAGNA
- 27 - HOME MADE PIZZA

## 07 - CAKES & BAKES
- 28 - PEACH COBBLER
- 29 - PANCAKES
- 30 - BROWNIES

# The Psychological Benefits of Eating Together as a Family

In today's technology-driven world, it can be challenging to balance work, bills, and family life. However, building a supportive relationship with our loved ones, especially children, is essential for their development and future success. According to Patrick Bailey, a professional writer in the field of mental health, addiction, and recovery, eating dinner together as a family can have a tremendous impact on children's psychological well-being.

Sharing a meal with loved ones can cultivate a relationship that lasts a lifetime. Casual dinner conversations can lead to problem-solving, idea sharing, and social interactions, resulting in essential life lessons. Children who regularly dine with family develop better life skills and mental abilities than those who do not.

Spending quality time at home with family can help prevent depression, isolation, and substance abuse, especially when parents are away at work. By providing a supportive and loving environment, children have someone to talk to and share their feelings and ideas with.

Overall, dining together as a family can have physical and mental positive benefits for children. Parents who understand the importance of family time have been making strides to spend more time at home together.

Adolescents are vulnerable to risky behavior when left unattended. Dining with family can assist with mental issues that may arise through conversation at dinner time. According to research done by the National Center on Addiction and Substance Abuse advise children who lack quality with family at the dinner table are more likely to engage in cigarette and marijuana smoking and alcohol use.

Parents who want to raise their children to be mentally savvy is worth putting forth the effort to eat and cook together. There are many opportunities in the kitchen to develop and create an environment that values communication, team work, problem solving and also an environment that values success. This success will not only be reflected in their schooling, skills and talents, but their overall quality of life.

Some helpful ways to begin connecting with your children if you are not normally able to eat together is as easy as planning one meal a week to eat together. Schedule eating time when time permits, parents can gradually increase the number of times the family dines together during the week. The more time spent together cooking and engaging together, the more comfortable and easier it will get for both parent and child to openly discuss their daily life challenges.

# The Importance of Family Mealtime and Its Positive Impact on Children

Mealtimes serve as an excellent opportunity for family members to connect with each other. Research has shown that dining together has a significant impact on the way children feel love, safety, and security. Regular family dinners promote psychological maturity, confidence and create an environment that encourages open communication.

Family dinner is a perfect chance for parents to teach children about their core values, traditions, and culture. This time together can help children distinguish between right and wrong in the context of their family values. Moreover, children should be made to understand that their family is their first support system. They should never be ashamed or hesitate to share their feelings, and they should always be able to communicate their concerns safely during family time.

Teamwork in the kitchen while preparing meals can lead to more family time. Involving children in grocery shopping, meal planning, and meal preparation can be a good learning experience that helps with their decision-making skills as adults. Even children who are new to the kitchen can participate by doing tasks such as taking food out of the refrigerator, sprinkling spices on food, washing fruits and vegetables, and preparing the dining table.

When children participate in meal preparation, their brains become more active, and parents get an opportunity to interact with and better understand their children. So, make it a point to have regular family meals and to involve everyone in preparing them.

# The Family Dinner Table: Cultivating Healthy Eating Habits and Positive Values in Children

Parents and other adult figures in a child's life serve as role models. Children tend to emulate the behaviors of adults around them, which is why it's important to set a good example. Research has shown that healthy eating habits are linked to a healthy mental state. Encouraging your children to eat healthily can have a positive impact on their mental capacity and overall well-being. On the other hand, denying them a nutritious diet can cause mental fatigue and poor decision-making. To prevent this, strive to incorporate a variety of fruits and vegetables into your family's meals.

Family dinner time can serve various purposes depending on each family's values and traditions. Some may use it as an opportunity to teach children table manners, while others may focus on communication and mutual respect. Regardless of the objective, regular family meals provide a chance for parents to connect with their children, understand their wants and needs, and instill positive values that will guide them as they grow into adults. This close interaction also allows parents to address any problems their children may be facing at school or home, promoting both physical and mental growth.

Teaching Kids to Cook: A Guide to Making Kitchen Time Fun and Productive

From as young as four years old, children learn to follow instructions and replicate tasks. This is the perfect time to start training them on delegating tasks. Children can take on redundant tasks such as cutting soft vegetables like steamed broccoli or peeling potatoes. Not only does this lighten your load, but it also builds their confidence and teaches them about kitchen safety.

Kids love the kitchen because it makes them feel important and grown-up. As they grow older, you'll find yourself needing to do less as they become more comfortable around kitchen tools and food. Each cooking lesson level has appropriate tasks per age, so your child can learn and grow at their own pace. Cleaning up can also be a delegated task, and making it fun can remove a big part of the stress. Have one child wipe scraps into the trash while the other rinses plates to hand to you.

Cooking with your kids can be an extremely joyous and fun time. It takes a little planning, the right tools, and a good attitude, but it's achievable. Give your little ones a peeler and a task, and watch as your stress levels peel off like a potato. Sometimes, it's difficult to get kids interested in the kitchen. However, the kitchen is a great place for kids to try new things, get creative, and have fun. Though some experiments may fail, discussing what happened and why it happened will help kids learn and grow.

The once-elusive domain of the kitchen is now within reach for kids. Allowing them to play and experiment in the kitchen is exciting and fun. If you want to inspire kids, give them the opportunity to play in the one area they were previously banned from entering.

Encouraging Kids to Explore the Kitchen and Develop Critical Thinking Skills

Cooking can be a fun and educational activity for children. With proper instruction on safety, kids can get creative and try new things in the kitchen. Even if experiments don't go as planned, adults have the opportunity to discuss what happened and why it happened. Here are some tips to keep kids engaged in the kitchen:

- Let them experiment: Kids love to play around and the kitchen is a great place to do just that. Allowing them to explore an area that was previously off-limits can be exciting and educational.
- Let them ask questions: Children are naturally curious and asking questions is a great way for them to learn. Adults should be prepared to answer questions and can even ask questions back to encourage critical thinking skills.
- Make time for discussion: Taking time to sit down and discuss what happened in the kitchen can keep kids interested and foster stronger bonds. It also helps them develop important critical thinking skills.

Encouraging children to explore the kitchen not only teaches them valuable life skills, but also helps them develop confidence and creativity.

Encouraging Kids to Cook: Tips for Getting Them Interested

If you want to get your kids interested in cooking, the key is to let them take the reins. Although it may make some adults uneasy, giving children the space to try tasks on their own is a great way to spark their curiosity. They can ask for help when they need it, but the chance to get hands-on is invaluable.

Kids love to experiment and play, especially when there are no strict rules to follow. Letting them discover new techniques, such as using a mixer instead of a fork, or slowly pouring flour to avoid sneezing, can be a fun way to introduce them to the kitchen.

By giving them the freedom to ask questions and try new things, you can easily pique their interest in cooking. The best way to keep them engaged is to get in the kitchen with them, relax, and enjoy the experience. So why not grab your kids, head to the kitchen, and have some fun cooking together?

(DEBBIE MADSON)

# 01
SOUPS AND STARTERS

DIVE INTO A SENSORY FEAST WITH OUR MAGICAL SOUP CONCOCTIONS! FEELING A HANKERING FOR A HUG IN A BOWL? INDULGE IN THE FLAVORFUL UNIVERSE OF OUR HANDCRAFTED TACO SOUP OR THE CALMING VEGETABLE SOUP. YOUR TASTE BUDS ARE IN FOR A TREAT!

## QUICK & EASY
# TACO SOUP

# Recipe

GROUND BEEF
BEEF BROTH
ROTEL
KIDNEY BEANS
BLACK BEANS
SWEET CORN
CILANTRO
ONION
GARLIC
TACO SAUCE
TOMATO SAUCE
SEASONINGS OF YOUR PREFERENCE

1. PLACE A LITTLE EVOO IN A PAN AND ADD ONIONS AND 3-4 MINCED GARLIC CLOVES IN AND COOK UNTIL ONIONS ARE TRANSLUCENT
2. SEASON AND GROUND BEEF UNTIL DONE, DRAIN OFF GREASE AND COMBINE WITH ONIONS AND GARLIC.
3. ADD ROTEL (ADJUST DEPENDING ON SIZE OF POT)
4. ADD HEAPING TBS OF TOMATO PASTE.
5. ADD IN TACO SAUCE AND TACO SEASONING PACKET TO YOUR DESIRED LIKING
6. ADD IN BEEF BROTH (32OZ)
7. ADD BEANS OF CHOICE, ( LIGHT RED, DARK RED, BLACK BEAN, PINTO) OR COMBINATION OF ALL.
8. ADD IN FRESH SWEET CORN
SIMMER ON MEDIUM LOW HEAT FOR 30 MIN. AND ENJOY WITH CHIPS OR CRACKERS OF YOUR CHOICE.

# *Thoughts*

## TACO SOUP CAN BE MADE AS A VEGAN OPTION.

This flavorful soup is a great way to enjoy a warm and hearty meal, even if you're following a vegan diet. To make it vegan-friendly, simply swap out the ground beef for a plant-based alternative, such as crumbled tofu, tempeh, or textured vegetable protein. You can also use vegetable broth instead of beef broth, and ensure that all other ingredients are vegan-friendly. Some great additions to this soup include diced tomatoes, corn, black beans, and a variety of spices like chili powder, cumin, and paprika. Whether you're a vegan or just looking for a delicious and healthy meal, Taco Soup is a great choice that's sure to satisfy your cravings.

# HOT & COMFORATING
# VEGETABLE SOUP

02

# Recipe

- 3 TABLESPOONS OLIVE OIL
- 2 TABLESPOONS GHEE OR UNSALTED BUTTER
- 2 LEEKS (WHITE PART ONLY), QUARTERED AND SLICED THINLY
- 3 CARROTS, PEELED AND DICED SMALL
- 3 PARSNIPS, PEELED AND DICED SMALL
- 3 RIBS CELERY, DICED SMALL
- 2 SMALL RED POTATOES, PEELED AND DICED SMALL
- SALT
- BLACK PEPPER
- 1 TEASPOONS DRIED PARSLEY
- 1 TEASPOON ITALIAN SEASONING
- 4 CLOVES GARLIC, PRESSED THROUGH GARLIC PRESS
- 1 (14.5 OUNCE) CAN WHOLE TOMATOES, DRAINED AND SEEDED, AND FINELY DICED
- 6 CUPS VEGETABLES BROTH OR CHICKEN BROTH
- 1 CUP PEAS
- 1 CUP KALE, CHOPPED
- 1 TABLESPOON CHOPPED, FRESH PARSLEY
- SMALL SQUEEZE OF LEMON

1. BEGIN BY GATHERING AND PREPPING ALL OF YOUR INGREDIENTS ACCORDING TO THE INGREDIENT LIST ABOVE TO HAVE READY AND ORGANIZED FOR USE.
2. PLACE A MEDIUM-LARGE SOUP POT OVER MEDIUM-HIGH HEAT, AND ADD IN THE GHEE OR BUTTER AND THE OIL. ONCE MELTED TOGETHER, ADD IN THE LEEKS, CARROTS, PARSNIPS, CELERY AND DICED POTATOES, PLUS A PINCH OR TWO OF SALT AND BLACK PEPPER, AND COOK THOSE TOGETHER FOR ABOUT 3-4 MINUTES, OR UNTIL THEY BEGIN TO BECOME SLIGHTLY TRANSLUCENT.
3. ADD THE ITALIAN SEASONING AND THE DRIED PARSLEY, ALONG WITH THE GARLIC, AND STIR THOSE IN TO INCORPORATE.
4. THEN, ADD THE TOMATOES FOLLOWED BY THE VEGETABLE OR CHICKEN STOCK, AND BRING TO THE BOIL. ONCE BOILING, REDUCE THE HEAT SO THAT THE SOUP IS GENTLY SIMMERING, COVER, AND ALLOW TO COOK FOR 15 MINUTES, OR UNTIL THE VEGETABLES ARE TENDER YET HAVE A SLIGHT BITE STILL.
5. TURN THE HEAT OFF THE SOUP, STIR IN THE PEAS, KALE, CHOPPED PARSLEY AND THE SMALL SQUEEZE OF LEMON, AND TASTE TO SEE IF ANY ADDITIONAL SALT/PEPPER IS NEEDED BEFORE SERVING.

# *thoughts*

Vegetables soup can be made with all types of ingredients. Don't limit yourself to the basic vegetables we always see, get creative and have fun experimenting and learning about different veggies with your family.

Some popular vegetables you can use to make soup include carrots, celery, onions, potatoes, and tomatoes. You can also add in some leafy greens like spinach or kale for extra nutrition. If you're foeeling adventurous, try adding in some less-familiar veggies like parsnips, turnips, or rutabagas. These root vegetables can add a unique flavor and texture to your soup. Don't forget to season your soup with herbs and spices to enhance the flavors even more. With a little bit of creativity and experimentation, you can whip up a delicious and healthy vegetable soup that your whole family will love.

COMFORTING
# CHICKEN SOUP

# Recipe

Chicken soup is a classic and comforting dish that is perfect for cold winter days or when you're feeling under the weather. This recipe is easy to follow and uses simple ingredients that you probably already have in your kitchen.

Ingredients:

- 1 whole chicken, cut into pieces
- 4 carrots, chopped
- 3 celery stalks, chopped
- 1 onion, chopped
- 4 garlic cloves, minced
- 2 bay leaves
- 1 teaspoon dried thyme
- 8 cups chicken broth
- Salt and pepper, to taste
- 1 cup egg noodles
- Avocado (my favorite)

Instructions:

1. In a large pot, heat up some oil over medium heat and add the chopped onion, celery, and carrots. Cook until the vegetables are softened, about 10 minutes.
2. Add the minced garlic, bay leaves, and dried thyme. Stir for a minute or two, until fragrant.
3. Add the chicken pieces and pour in the chicken broth. Season with salt and pepper to taste.
4. Bring the soup to a boil, then reduce the heat and let it simmer for 45 minutes to an hour.
5. Remove the chicken pieces from the soup and shred the meat. Discard the bones and set the meat aside.
6. Add the egg noodles to the soup and cook until tender, about 8-10 minutes.
7. Return the shredded chicken to the soup, adjust the seasoning if necessary, and serve hot.

This chicken soup recipe is not only delicious but also a great way to nourish your body with healthy ingredients. Enjoy!

# thoughts

Chicken soup is a great option especially when its cold outside. Maybe your children have gotten a cold, this recipe will surely help them feel better.

Chicken soup is not only delicious but also contains many health benefits. It is packed with nutrients that can help boost the immune system and fight off colds and flu. The warm broth can also help soothe sore throats and relieve congestion. In addition, chicken soup is easy to digest, making it a great option for those who are feeling under the weather. So next time you or a loved one is feeling sick, whip up a batch of homemade chicken soup and let its healing properties work their magic.

The Messy Chef's

# OVEN SHRIMP KABOBS

# Recipe

1 LB. LARGE SHRIMP, PEELED AND DEVEINED (YOU CAN LEAVE TAILS ON OR REMOVE THEM) FRESH SHRIMP OR FROZEN, 16-20 COUNT OR LARGER WORK BEST
1/4 CUP EXTRA VIRGIN OLIVE OIL
2 TSP HONEY
4 TBSP FRESH GARLIC, MINCED (ABOUT 4 CLOVES) (THE BEST GARLIC CHOPPER)
4 TABLESPOONS FRESH LEMON JUICE + ZEST FROM ONE LEMON
1 TBSP FRESH PARSLEY, FINELY CHOPPED
1 TSP SEA SALT OR KOSHER SALT
FRESHLY GROUND BLACK PEPPER, TO TASTE
RED PEPPER FLAKES, OPTIONAL IF YOU WANT A LITTLE HEAT

1. IN A MEDIUM BOWL, WHISK TOGETHER INGREDIENTS FOR THE SHRIMP MARINADE: OLIVE OIL, HONEY, LEMON JUICE + LEMON ZEST, SALT, GARLIC, PARSLEY AND A FEW GRINDS OF FRESHLY GROUND PEPPER AND RED PEPPER FLAKES (OPTIONAL). **SPOON OUT A COUPLE OF TABLESPOONS OF THE MARINADE AND SET ASIDE FOR DRIZZLING LATER**
2. ADD SHRIMP TO THE REMAINING MARINADE AND TOSS REALLY WELL UNTIL ALL SHRIMP ARE COATED IN THE MARINADE. LET SHRIMP MARINATE FOR 20-30 MINUTES. (PRO TIP: WHILE SHRIMP IS MARINATING, THIS IS WHEN I LIKE TO PREPARE ANY SIDES SUCH AS RICE OR A SALAD. ONCE THE SHRIMP GO INTO THE OVEN, THEY ARE DONE SUPER QUICKLY!)
3. PREHEAT OVEN TO 450°F. THREAD SHRIMP ONTO BAMBOO SKEWERS (METAL SKEWERS WORK, TOO), PUTTING ABOUT 4-6 SHRIMP ON EACH SKEWER, DEPENDING ON THEIR SIZE. PLACE SKEWERS ON A LARGE BAKING SHEET LINED WITH ALUMINUM FOIL OR PARCHMENT PAPER FOR EASY CLEAN UP (YOU CAN ALSO JUST SPRAY YOUR SHEET PAN WITH COOKING SPRAY).
4. ROAST SHRIMP FOR 3-4 MINUTES UNTIL SHRIMP HAVE JUST STARTED TO TURN BRIGHT PINK AND THERE ARE NO GRAY (RAW!) SPOTS (SEE NOTE 1). DRIZZLE WITH RESERVED MARINADE AND SERVE WITH EXTRA LEMON WEDGES!

# *thoughts*

Delicious Oven Baked Shrimp Skewers Recipe with Vegan and Fruity Options

Looking for a quick and easy shrimp recipe that's packed with flavor? Look no further than these oven-baked shrimp skewers! Bursting with zesty lemon, fresh garlic, and herbs, these skewers are a perfect meal for hectic weeknights.

For a vegan twist, switch out the shrimp for oyster, portabella, or shiitake mushrooms. For an extra fruity touch, add some juicy pineapples to create a Hawaiian-inspired grilled shrimp kabob.

If you prefer your food with a little heat, add some hot sauce or tabasco to the marinade.

# The Messy Chef Nachos

# Recipe

Nachos are a popular snack that's perfect for movie nights, game days, or just a simple get-together with family and friends. Making nachos at home is not only easy but also allows you to customize the toppings to your liking. Here is a simple nacho recipe and a list of ingredients that you can use to make your very own delicious nachos.

Ingredients:

- Tortilla chips
- Shredded cheese (cheddar, Monterey Jack, or a mix)
- Black beans
- Diced tomatoes
- Sliced jalapeños
- Sour cream
- Guacamole

Directions:

1. Preheat your oven to 350°F.
2. Spread a layer of tortilla chips on a baking sheet.
3. Sprinkle shredded cheese over the chips.
4. Add a layer of black beans, diced tomatoes, and sliced jalapeños.
5. Repeat the layers until all ingredients are used up.
6. Bake in the oven for 10-15 minutes, or until the cheese is melted and bubbly.
7. Remove from the oven and let cool for a few minutes.
8. Serve with a dollop of sour cream and guacamole on top.

Enjoy your homemade nachos with your favorite beverage, and don't forget to share with your family and friends!

# thoughts

Some of us don't do well with dairy products, but we still want the enjoyment of some great cheesy nachos. There are various vegan cheese options that can be used to substitute dairy cheese.

Vegan cheese is made from plant-based ingredients and can be just as delicious as dairy cheese. Some popular vegan cheese options include cashew cheese, almond cheese, and soy cheese. These alternatives not only provide a great taste, but they're are also much healthier than traditional cheese. They are usually lower in calories, fat, and cholesterol, making them a great alternative for those who are watching their diet. So next time you're craving some cheesy nachos, try using a vegan cheese substitute and enjoy the same great taste without any of the dairy.

# 02
## SALADS

SOMETIMES YOU'RE IN THE MOOD FOR A LIGHT MEAL, AND THAT'S WHEN YOU NEED SOME DELICIOUS SALAD RECIPES.
WE HAVE PLENTY OF SATISFYING, FLAVORFUL SALADS HERE AT THE MESSY CHEF, FROM GLAZED SALMON SALAD, GRILLED CHICKEN SALAD AND YOU CAN'T HAVE A COOKOUT WITH OUR MESSY COBB <u>SALAD</u> AND GREEN <u>FLUFF SALAD</u>!

# GLAZED SALMON SALAD

DR. APRIL A. JONES

o6

# Recipe

If you're looking for a healthy and delicious meal, try making a glazed salmon salad. To make this dish, you'll need some fresh salmon fillets, mixed greens, cherry tomatoes, cucumber, red onion, and a few other ingredients. I add mandarin oranges to mine.

For the salmon, mix together some soy sauce, honey, garlic, and ginger in a bowl. Place the salmon fillets on a baking sheet and brush the glaze over the top. Bake in the oven for about 15-20 minutes, or until the salmon is cooked through.

While the salmon is cooking, prepare the salad. Wash and dry the mixed greens and place them in a large bowl. Slice the cherry tomatoes in half and add them to the bowl, along with sliced cucumber and red onion.

Once the salmon is done, let it cool for a few minutes and then flake it into bite-sized pieces. Add the salmon to the salad and toss everything together.

For the dressing, whisk together some olive oil, lemon juice, Dijon mustard, and a pinch of salt and pepper. Drizzle the dressing over the salad and serve immediately.

This glazed salmon salad is a perfect dish for a quick lunch or a light dinner. It's packed with protein and healthy greens, and the combination of flavors is sure to impress. Give it a try and see for yourself!

# thoughts

Salmon isn't just a fish, it's a superhero meal for your little ones! Packed with omega-3 goodness for super smart brains and muscles of steel, this fishy delight is a top pick for growing champs. Serving up salmon to the kiddos not only fuels their growth but also introduces them to a world of tasty and healthy eats. Whether it's grilled, baked, or sizzled in a pan, there are endless ways to dish up salmon that'll make the little munchkins jump for joy!

# Grilled Chicken Salad

*Classic Salad* 07

# Recipe

If you're looking for a healthy and delicious meal option, a grilled chicken salad is a great choice. Here are the ingredients you'll need:

- Boneless, skinless chicken breasts
- Mixed salad greens
- Cherry tomatoes
- Cucumber
- Red onion
- Avocado
- Feta cheese
- Lemon
- Olive oil
- Salt and pepper

To make the salad, begin by grilling the chicken breasts until fully cooked. Let them cool for a few minutes before slicing them into strips. While the chicken is cooking, wash and chop the salad greens, cherry tomatoes, cucumber, and red onion. Cut the avocado into small pieces and crumble the feta cheese.

Arrange the salad greens on a large platter or individual plates. Add the sliced chicken, cherry tomatoes, cucumber, red onion, avocado, and feta cheese on top. Squeeze fresh lemon juice over the salad and drizzle with olive oil. Sprinkle with salt and pepper to taste.

Enjoy your delicious and nutritious grilled chicken salad!

# thoughts

Substitute the grilled chicken on this salad for vegan options.

Eating a plant-based diet has become increasingly popular as more people become aware of the health and environmental benefits. Restaurants and cafes have taken notice and are offering more vegan options on their menus.

If you're someone who prefers a vegan lifestyle or simply want to try something new, you can now substitute the grilled chicken in your salad with a variety of vegan options. Some popular substitutes include tofu, tempeh, chickpeas, and seitan. These options are not only delicious but also provide a good source of protein that will keep you energized throughout the day.

# MESSY COBB SALADS

# Recipe

Cobb Salad is a classic American salad that is both delicious and healthy. This salad is made with a variety of ingredients that come together to create a perfect balance of flavors. The ingredients typically include chopped lettuce, hard-boiled eggs, avocado, tomatoes, bacon, chicken, and blue cheese.

To make the salad, start by arranging a bed of chopped lettuce on a plate. Then, add sliced hard-boiled eggs, diced avocado, sliced tomatoes, crumbled bacon, and diced chicken on top of the lettuce. Finally, sprinkle crumbled blue cheese over the salad.

For the dressing, you can use a classic vinaigrette or a creamy dressing like ranch or blue cheese. Whichever dressing you choose, be sure to drizzle it over the salad just before serving.

Cobb Salad is a great meal option for lunch or dinner. It is packed with protein, healthy fats, and vegetables, making it a nutritious and filling option. Plus, it is easy to customize by adding or subtracting ingredients based on your personal preferences.

# *thoughts*

## Cobb Salads

are classic American salads that's been around since the 1930s. The salad typically consists of chopped lettuce, tomatoes, chicken breast, bacon, hard-boiled eggs, avocado, and Roquefort cheese. The toppings are arranged in rows on top of the lettuce, which makes for an attractive presentation. The salad is usually served with a vinaigrette dressing on the side, but some people prefer a creamy blue cheese dressing instead. The Cobb salad is a hearty and filling meal that's perfect for lunch or dinner. It's also a great way to use up leftover chicken or bacon. If you're looking to switch up your salad game, give the Cobb salad a try!

# GREEN FLUFF SALAD

DR. APRIL A. JONES

09

 # Recipe

To make a delicious green leafy salad, you'll need a variety of fresh ingredients. Start with a base of mixed greens, such as spinach, arugula, and romaine lettuce. Add some crunch with sliced cucumbers, carrots, and radishes. For a burst of sweetness, add cherry tomatoes and sliced strawberries.

Next, it's time to whip up a dressing. A simple vinaigrette made with olive oil, balsamic vinegar, Dijon mustard, and honey is a great place to start. Whisk all the ingredients together until emulsified and drizzle over the salad to taste.

For a heartier salad, add some protein such as grilled chicken or shrimp, hard-boiled eggs, or crumbled feta cheese. Top it off with some roasted nuts or seeds for added texture and flavor.

With these ingredients and recipe, you'll have a delicious and healthy green leafy salad that's perfect for any meal of the day. Enjoy!

# thoughts

Green leafy vegetables mixed together in a salad provide a range of essential vitamins and minerals that are vital for maintaining good health. These vegetables are packed full of nutrients such as vitamin A, C, K, and folate, which are important for healthy skin, vision, and immune function. Additionally, they are rich in fiber, which helps to support healthy digestion and can aid in weight management. Some examples of green leafy vegetables that can be included in a salad are spinach, kale, arugula, and romaine lettuce. To make your salad even more nutritious, try adding some lean protein such as grilled chicken or tofu, and healthy fats such as avocado or nuts. A colorful and delicious green salad is a great way to nourish your body and support overall health and wellbeing.

# O3
## SEAFOOD

**STRONG EVIDENCE HAS SHOWN THAT EATING FISH AND OTHER SEAFOODS IMPROVE BRAIN, EYE, AND HEART HEALTH. THE NEW 2020-2025 DIETARY GUIDELINES FOR AMERICANS (DGA) RECOMMEND THAT AMERICANS OF ALL AGES SHOULD EAT MORE SEAFOOD—AT LEAST TWICE A WEEK—PARTICULARLY PREGNANT WOMEN AND YOUNG CHILDREN.**

*Chengchu Liu*  *Nicholas V C Ralston*

# CAJUN SEAFOOD HOBO POUCHES

BY GWENDOLYN JONES

# Recipe

## INGREDIENTS

GARLIC CLOVES (MINCED) FRESH EARS OF CORN (DESIRED AMOUNT) BABY RED OR GOLD POTATOES WHITE OR YELLOW ONIONS (TO YOUR PREFERENCE) RED, GREEN AND YELLOW BELL PEPPERS SHRIMP CAJUN AUDOILLE SAUSAUGE TONY'S CREOLE SEASONING OLD BAY SEASONING GARLIC POWDER BLACK PEPPER CRUSHED RED PEPPER FLAKES BUTTER

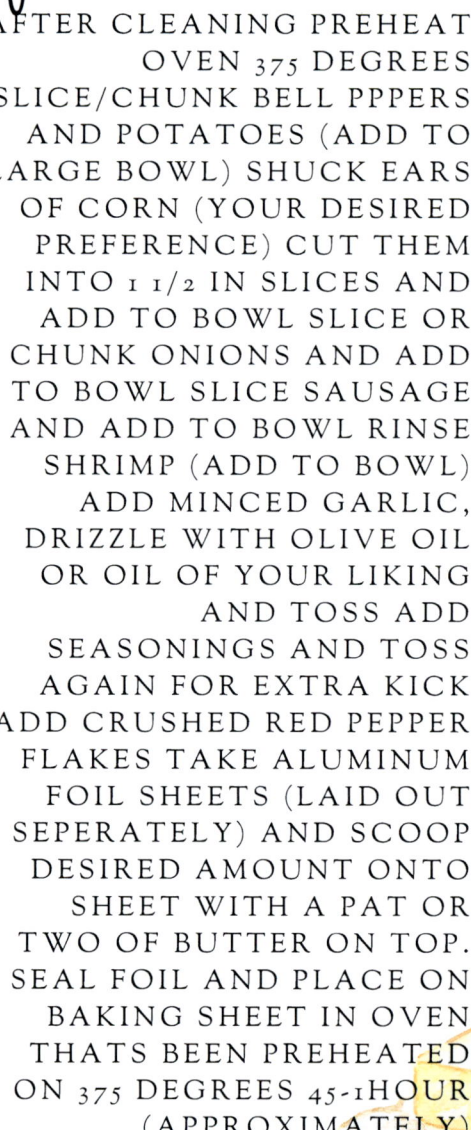

AFTER CLEANING PREHEAT OVEN 375 DEGREES SLICE/CHUNK BELL PPPERS AND POTATOES (ADD TO LARGE BOWL) SHUCK EARS OF CORN (YOUR DESIRED PREFERENCE) CUT THEM INTO 1 1/2 IN SLICES AND ADD TO BOWL SLICE OR CHUNK ONIONS AND ADD TO BOWL SLICE SAUSAGE AND ADD TO BOWL RINSE SHRIMP (ADD TO BOWL) ADD MINCED GARLIC, DRIZZLE WITH OLIVE OIL OR OIL OF YOUR LIKING AND TOSS ADD SEASONINGS AND TOSS AGAIN FOR EXTRA KICK ADD CRUSHED RED PEPPER FLAKES TAKE ALUMINUM FOIL SHEETS (LAID OUT SEPERATELY) AND SCOOP DESIRED AMOUNT ONTO SHEET WITH A PAT OR TWO OF BUTTER ON TOP. SEAL FOIL AND PLACE ON BAKING SHEET IN OVEN THATS BEEN PREHEATED ON 375 DEGREES 45-1HOUR (APPROXIMATELY)

# *Thoughts*

## TAKE CAUTION WHEN COOKING SEAFOOD AND CHECK FOR ALLERGIES.

Seafood is a delicious and healthy source of protein, but it's important to handle it with care when cooking. One of the biggest risks associated with cooking seafood is the potential for allergic reactions. It's essential to take precautions to ensure that your guests or loved ones are not exposed to any allergens. Some common seafood allergens include shrimp, crab, and lobster. If you're not sure about someone's dietary restrictions, it's always best to err on the side of caution and avoid cooking seafood altogether. However, if you do choose to cook seafood, make sure to properly clean and prepare it to avoid any contamination. By following these tips, you can safely enjoy the delicious taste of seafood while keeping yourself and others safe from harm.

# SAC FRIED FISH SANDWICH

DR. APRIL A. JONES

11

# Recipe

There's no taste quite like that of a crispy and mouthwatering fried fish sandwich. Here's how you can create your own at home with a few essential ingredients:

- Start with fresh white fish like cod, haddock, or tilapia.
- Prepare flour, cornmeal, or breadcrumbs for coating the fish before frying.
- Enhance the breading with a mix of herbs and spices like paprika, garlic powder, and cayenne pepper.
- Opt for high-quality oil like canola or vegetable oil for frying.
- Gather sandwich fixings such as lettuce, tomato, and tartar sauce to complement your sandwich.

To cook your sandwich:

1. Heat oil in a deep frying pan or fryer and coat the fish thoroughly with the flour or breadcrumb mixture.
2. Carefully fry the fish until it turns golden brown and crispy on the outside and tender on the inside.
3. Once fried, drain excess oil by placing the fish on a paper towel.

Assemble your sandwich:

- Place the fish on a bun or bread of your choice.
- Add your preferred sandwich fillings.
- Top it off with tartar sauce and savor your homemade fried fish sandwich!

# Thoughts

I use a premade batter instead of corn meal and season my fish with lemon pepper seasoning. I also prefer to use Swai fish for my sandwhiches. Everyone has a preference when it comes different kinds of fish they use.

When it comes to making a tasty fish sandwich, there are a few tips and tricks that can take your sandwich to the next level. Firstly, using a premade batter can save you time and ensure a consistent result every time. Additionally, seasoning your fish with lemon pepper can add a burst of zesty flavor that complements the fish perfectly.

As for the type of fish to use, it really comes down to personal preference. Some people prefer a firmer, meatier fish like cod or halibut, while others opt for a lighter, flakier fish like Swai or tilapia. Whatever your choice may be, make sure to choose a fish that is fresh and sustainably sourced for the best taste and ethical considerations.

Lastly, don't forget about the toppings! A fish sandwich is only as good as its fixings. Consider adding some fresh lettuce, tomato, and tartar sauce for a classic take, or experiment with different sauces and toppings to find your perfect combination. With these tips in mind, you'll be well on your way to making the ultimate fish sandwich.

# BAKED FISH

12

# Recipe

A Delicious and Healthy Meal in Minutes: Baked Fish with Lemon and Tomatoes Recipe

Are you searching for a nutritious and delicious meal that is easy and quick to prepare? Try this recipe for baked fish with lemon and tomatoes.
Here's how you can make it:

- Begin by preheating your oven to 375°F.
- Season the fish fillets with salt and pepper, and then place them in a baking dish.
- Add a layer of lemon slices and diced tomatoes on top of the fillets.
- Drizzle some olive oil over the ingredients.
- Bake it for 20-25 minutes until the fish is cooked through and the tomatoes are soft and fragrant.
- Serve it with roasted veggies or a fresh salad for a complete meal.

This dish is perfect for any occasion, whether it's a weeknight dinner or a special celebration. The tangy and zesty flavors of the lemon and tomato, combined with the tender and flaky fish, create a light yet satisfying meal.

# thoughts

Fish is a healthy source of protein and essential nutrients such as omega-3 fatty acids. However, the cooking method can greatly impact its nutritional value. Frying fish can add unwanted calories and unhealthy fats to your diet.

On the other hand, baking or grilling fish can preserve its nutritional content while adding flavor without the extra fat. So next time you're preparing fish for a meal, consider baking or grilling it for a healthier option.

# SEAFOOD BOIL

13

# Recipe

If you're looking for a delicious and easy seafood boil recipe, you can't go wrong with crab legs. Here are the ingredients you'll need to get started:

- 2 pounds of crab legs
- 1 pound of shrimp, peeled and deveined
- 1 pound of mussels
- 1 pound of clams
- 4 ears of corn, shucked and cut into thirds
- 1 pound of red potatoes, halved
- 1 onion, quartered
- 4 cloves of garlic, minced
- 2 lemons, halved
- 1/2 cup of Old Bay seasoning
- 1 stick of butter
- 5 cups of water

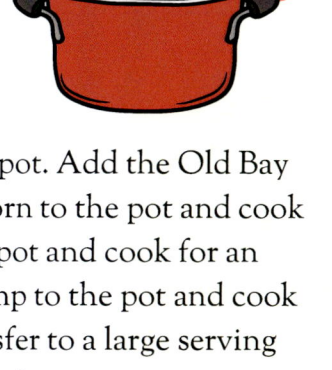

To make the seafood boil, start by bringing the water to a boil in a large pot. Add the Old Bay seasoning, garlic, and onion to the pot and stir. Add the potatoes and corn to the pot and cook for about 10 minutes. Next, add the crab legs, mussels, and clams to the pot and cook for an additional 5-7 minutes, or until the shells open up. Finally, add the shrimp to the pot and cook for 2-3 minutes, or until they turn pink. Drain the seafood boil and transfer to a large serving platter. Serve with the melted butter and lemon halves on the side. Enjoy!

# thoughts

Crab legs are a delicious seafood delicacy that is enjoyed by many people around the world. They are a popular dish often served in upscale restaurants and can be prepared in a variety of ways. Crab legs are usually served steamed or boiled and are often accompanied by melted butter or a tangy dipping sauce.

Crab legs are known for their sweet and succulent meat, which is why they are considered a delicacy. They are usually harvested from several species of crabs, including king crab, snow crab, and Dungeness crab. King crab legs are the largest and most sought after, while snow crab legs are smaller and more delicate.

When preparing crab legs, it is important to handle them gently to avoid breaking the delicate meat inside. They can be cooked in a large pot of boiling water or steamed in a steamer basket. Once cooked, they can be served with a variety of sides, such as roasted vegetables or a fresh salad.

Overall, crab legs are a delicious and healthy seafood option that is enjoyed by many. They are a great source of protein and are low in calories, making them a perfect addition to any meal. Whether you are dining out at a fancy restaurant or cooking at home, crab legs are sure to impress your guests and leave them feeling satisfied.

# 04

MEAT DISHES

EATING HEALTHY CAN BE CHALLENGING, BUT WITH THESE MOUTH-WATERING MEAT-BASED RECIPES, IT'S A BREEZE TO HAVE A BALANCED MEAL. OUR PASTA AND SAUSAGE, STUFFED PEPPERS, BACON BURGERS, MEATLOAF AND POTATOES, AND CRAZY TACOS RECIPES NOT ONLY PROVIDE PLENTY OF PROTEIN BUT ALSO INCORPORATE A VARIETY OF VEGETABLES.

# TURKEY MEATLOAF W/ HOMEMADE MASHED & GRAVY, POTATOES AND GREEN BEANS

DR. APRIL A. JONES

# Recipe

The key to making a delicious meatloaf is to use high-quality ingredients. Here are some of the must-have ingredients for a perfect meatloaf:

1. Ground beef: This is the star ingredient in meatloaf. Choose ground beef that is at least 80% lean and 20% fat for the juiciest meatloaf.
2. Bread crumbs: Bread crumbs are used as a binder to hold the meatloaf together. You can use fresh bread crumbs or dried bread crumbs, depending on your preference.
3. Eggs: Eggs also act as a binder in meatloaf. They add moisture and help the meatloaf hold its shape.
4. Milk: Milk is optional, but it can help make the meatloaf more tender and moist.
5. Onion: Onion adds flavor and moisture to the meatloaf. Make sure to chop the onion finely so it blends well with the other ingredients.
6. Garlic: Garlic is another flavor enhancer that can take your meatloaf to the next level. Use fresh garlic for the best flavor.
7. Worcestershire sauce: Worcestershire sauce adds a savory, umami flavor to the meatloaf. It is a must-have ingredient for any meatloaf recipe.
8. Salt and pepper: Salt and pepper are essential for seasoning the meatloaf. Be generous with the seasoning to bring out the flavors of the other ingredients.

With these ingredients, you can make a delicious meatloaf that everyone will love. Don't be afraid to experiment with different herbs and spices to customize your meatloaf to your taste. Enjoy!

Meatloaf and mashed potatoes is a classic American dish that has been enjoyed by many generations. This recipe is simple, hearty, and delicious, making it a perfect meal for any occasion.

To make the meatloaf, you will need ground beef, breadcrumbs, eggs, onion, garlic, ketchup, Worcestershire sauce, salt, and pepper. Mix all the ingredients together in a large bowl and shape them into a loaf. Place the meatloaf in a baking dish and bake in the oven for about an hour, or until the internal temperature reaches 160°F.

For the mashed potatoes, you will need potatoes, butter, milk, salt, and pepper. Peel and cut the potatoes into small pieces and boil them in a pot of water until they are soft. Drain the water and mash the potatoes with butter and milk until they are smooth and creamy. Add salt and pepper to taste.

Serve the meatloaf and mashed potatoes together on a plate and enjoy a delicious and comforting meal. You can also add some gravy or vegetables on the side to make it even more satisfying. This recipe is perfect for a family dinner or a cozy night in.

## thoughts

Onion soup mix can easily be used as the only seasoning thats needed in your meatloaf mix. I use one pack and it packs all the flavor I need to create the best meatloaf ever.

# STUFFED BELL PEPPERS

DR. APRIL A. JONES

# Recipe

Stuffed bell peppers are a hearty and delicious meal that can be enjoyed any time of the year. The ingredients you'll need for this recipe are:

- Bell peppers (any color you prefer)
- Ground beef or turkey (or a vegetarian protein source like lentils or tofu)
- Cooked rice
- Onion
- Garlic
- Tomato sauce
- Shredded cheese (optional)
- Salt and pepper to taste

To prepare the stuffed bell peppers, you'll need to first cut off the tops of the peppers and remove the seeds and membranes. Then, cook your protein source and rice according to their respective instructions. Sauté chopped onion and garlic in a pan until they are soft and fragrant. Mix the protein, rice, onion and garlic together in a bowl with tomato sauce and seasonings. Stuff the mixture into the bell peppers and top with shredded cheese if desired.

Bake the stuffed bell peppers in the oven until the peppers are tender and the cheese is melted and bubbly. Serve hot and enjoy!

## *thoughts*

Quick cheat tip, boil the bell peppers whole for five to seven minutes to soften them up before placing the ingredients inside them, then baked them!

# Recipe

If you're a fan of burgers, you know that the double bacon cheeseburger is the ultimate indulgence. To make this delicious burger at home, you'll need the following ingredients:

- 1 pound ground beef
- 4 slices of bacon
- 4 slices of cheddar cheese
- 4 hamburger buns
- Lettuce
- Tomato
- Onion
- Ketchup
- Mustard
- Salt
- Pepper

To start, cook the bacon in a pan until it's crispy. Remove from the pan and set aside. Divide the ground beef into four equal portions and shape each one into a patty. Season each patty with salt and pepper.

Heat up a grill or a grill pan over medium-high heat. Cook the burgers for about 3-4 minutes on each side, or until they reach your desired level of doneness. In the last minute of cooking, add a slice of cheddar cheese on top of each patty and let it melt.

While the burgers are cooking, prepare your toppings. Slice the tomato and onion and wash the lettuce leaves. Toast the hamburger buns.

To assemble the burgers, place a lettuce leaf on the bottom of each bun. Add a patty on top, followed by a slice of bacon, some tomato and onion slices, and a squirt of ketchup and mustard. Top with the other half of the bun.

Serve your double bacon cheeseburgers hot and enjoy the deliciousness!

# thoughts

Adding a fried egg to the cheeseburger can be a delicious way to elevate the flavors and textures of the classic burger. The runny yolk of the egg can create a rich and creamy sauce that blends perfectly with the melted cheese and savory beef. It also adds a layer of complexity to the dish, providing a contrast of textures between the crispy bacon, juicy meat, and soft bun. For those who prefer a bit of spice, adding a few slices of jalapenos or a drizzle of hot sauce can add a kick to this mouthwatering meal. Whether you're enjoying it at a restaurant or making it at home, a cheeseburger with a fried egg is a tasty and satisfying choice.

# Dr. Jones' CRAZY TACOS

How to Make Tacos: A Simple Guide

Tacos are a delicious and versatile meal that can be enjoyed any time of day. The beauty of tacos is that they can be personalized to suit your taste, with a variety of fillings and toppings to choose from. Here are some easy steps to make your very own:

- Start with a base of soft or hard tortillas, whichever you prefer.
- Choose your protein of choice: chicken, beef, pork, fish, or beans. Mix in some spices to add flavor and depth.
- Add your favorite toppings: sliced avocado, chopped tomato, shredded lettuce, diced onion, salsa, cheese, and sour cream.
- Warm up your tortillas, add your protein and toppings, roll them up, and you're ready to enjoy!

With this simple recipe and guide, you can create delicious and satisfying tacos in no time.

# thoughts

Tacos are a versatile dish that can be customized according to one's preferences and taste buds. From the type of meat to the toppings and sauces, you can make a taco any way you want. Some popular taco fillings include beef, chicken, pork, fish, and vegetables. You can also choose between hard or soft shells, or even opt for a lettuce wrap for a healthier option. Toppings can range from the classic shredded cheese, lettuce, and tomatoes to more unique options like pickled onions, guacamole, and salsa. And let's not forget about the sauces - from mild to spicy, there's a sauce for every taco lover. So go ahead and experiment with different combinations to create the perfect taco for you.

# Salmon Croquette with Southern Home Potatoes and Scrambled Eggs

Salmon croquettes are a delicious and easy way to enjoy leftover cooked salmon. To make them, simply mix together cooked salmon, breadcrumbs, eggs, and seasonings, then shape into patties and fry until golden brown. Serve them alongside scrambled eggs and crispy potatoes for a hearty and satisfying breakfast or brunch. The rich and savory flavors of the salmon croquettes pair perfectly with the light and fluffy scrambled eggs, while the crispy potatoes add a satisfying crunch.

# Recipe

- PANKO BREAD CRUMBS: THE BREADCRUMBS HELP TO FORM THE PERFECT CRUST.
- FLOUR: I USED ALL-PURPOSE FLOUR IN THIS RECIPE.
- BELL PEPPERS: THESE ARE OPTIONAL, BUT I LOVE THE ADDED COLOR, CRUNCH, AND FLAVOR THEY BRING TO THE CROQUETTES.
- CANNED SALMON: USING CANNED SALMON SAVES SO MUCH TIME!
- GARLIC POWDER: THIS IS SO DELICIOUS WITH THE SALMON.
- SALT AND PEPPER: THESE ENHANCE ALL OF THE FLAVORS IN THE RECIPE.
- EGG: THE EGG BINDS ALL OF THE INGREDIENTS TOGETHER MAKING IT EASY TO FORM PATTIES.
- MAYONNAISE: THIS ALSO HELPS BIND THE INGREDIENTS TOGETHER AND ADDS A CREAMINESS TO THE BASE.
- WORCESTERSHIRE SAUCE: THIS ADDED FLAVOR IS OUT OF THIS WORLD!
- FRESH CILANTRO: IF YOU AREN'T A FAN OF CILANTRO (IT SEEMS TO BE A LOVE-IT-OR-HATE-IT INGREDIENT), THEN YOU CAN LEAVE IT OUT!
- VEGETABLE OIL: I USE THE OIL TO COOK THE CROQUETTES IN THE SKILLET. IT HELPS THEM GET THAT GOLDEN BROWN COLOR.

# thoughts

For a healthier twist on this classic recipe, try using almond flour or ground flaxseed instead of breadcrumbs, and bake the croquettes in the oven instead of frying them. You can also add in other ingredients like chopped bell pepper, celery, or jalapeno for an extra kick of flavor. Enjoy!

# PINTO BEAN CHILI

DR. APRIL A. JONES

# Recipe

## INGREDIENTS

- 1 POUND DRIED PINTO BEANS
- 2 POUNDS GROUND BEEF
- 1 MEDIUM ONION, CHOPPED
- 3 CELERY RIBS, CHOPPED
- 3 TABLESPOONS ALL-PURPOSE FLOUR
- 4 CUPS WATER
- 2 TABLESPOONS CHILI POWDER
- 2 TABLESPOONS GROUND CUMIN
- 1/2 TEASPOON SUGAR
- 1 CAN (28 OUNCES) CRUSHED TOMATOES
- 2 TEASPOONS CIDER VINEGAR
- 1-1/2 TEASPOONS SALT
- OPTIONAL: CORN OFF THE COB, CHOPPED RED ONION, SLICED JALAPENO PEPPER AND SOUR CREAM

## INSTRUCTIONS

PLACE BEANS IN A DUTCH OVEN OR SOUP KETTLE; ADD WATER TO COVER BY 2 IN. BRING TO A BOIL; BOIL FOR 2 MINUTES. REMOVE FROM THE HEAT; COVER AND LET STAND FOR 1 HOUR. DRAIN AND RINSE BEANS, DISCARDING LIQUID.

1. IN A DUTCH OVEN, COOK THE BEEF, ONION AND CELERY OVER MEDIUM HEAT UNTIL MEAT IS NO LONGER PINK; DRAIN. STIR IN FLOUR UNTIL BLENDED. GRADUALLY STIR IN WATER. ADD THE BEANS, CHILI POWDER, CUMIN AND SUGAR. BRING TO A BOIL. REDUCE HEAT; COVER AND SIMMER FOR 1-1/2 HOURS OR UNTIL BEANS ARE TENDER. STIR IN THE TOMATOES, VINEGAR AND SALT; HEAT THROUGH, STIRRING OCCASIONALLY. IF DESIRED, SERVE WITH OPTIONAL TOPPINGS.

## *thoughts*

Top your pinto bean chili with the classic toppings like sour cream, shredded cheese, cilantro and tortilla chips. Yes, you can use canned pinto beans for this recipe. Add more spice by increasing the amount of cumin and chili powder. You could also add sliced jalapenos to add some more zip.

# 05
## DESSERTS

TO INCORPORATE DESSERTS INTO A HEALTHY DIET, CHOOSE OPTIONS WITH MINIMAL ADDED SUGAR AND KEEP PORTIONS SMALL.

# Candied Popcorn

Gwendolyn Jones

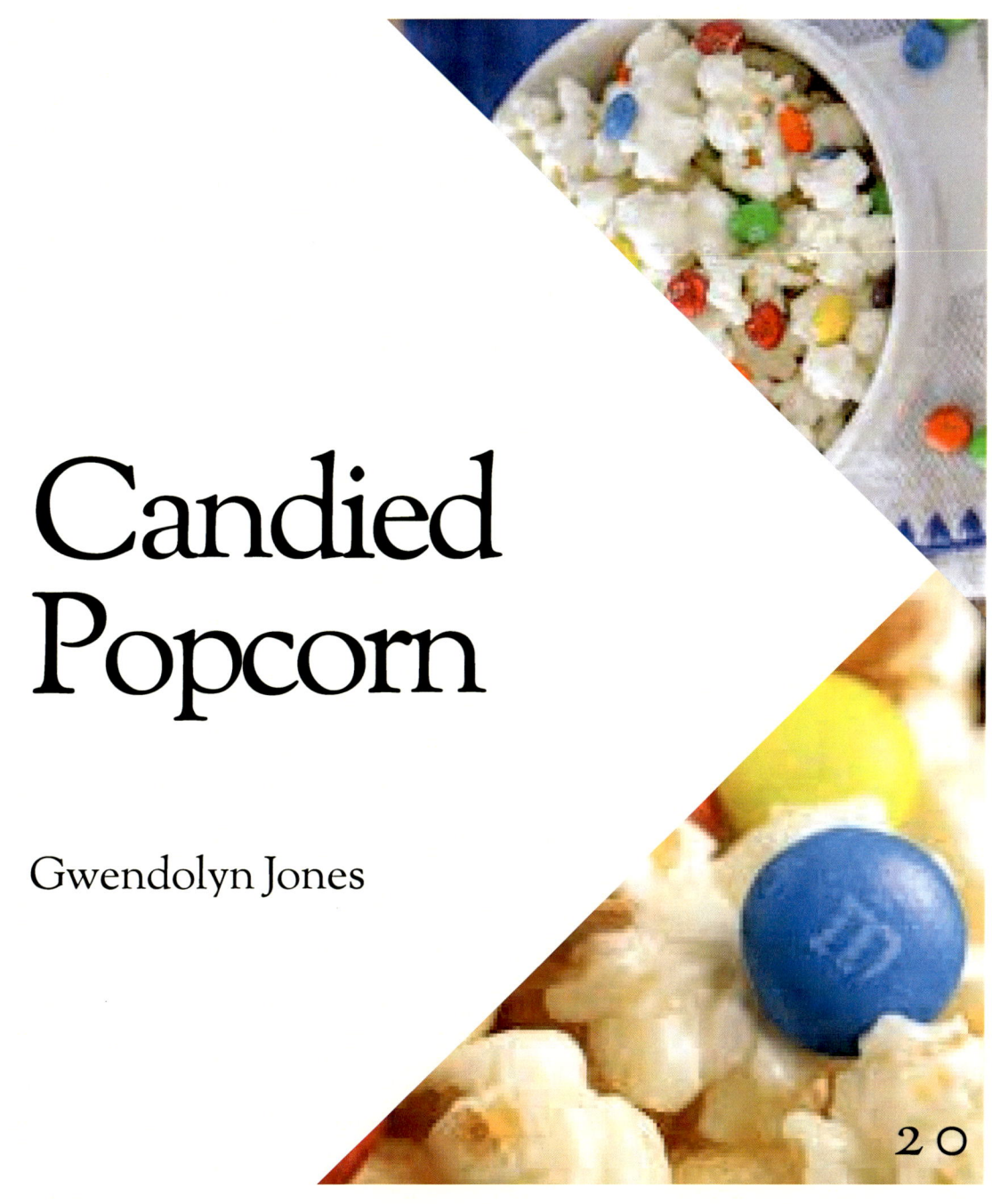

# Recipe

## INGREDIENTS

- TIN OF POPCORN
- ALMOND BARK - (WHITE)
- RED AND GREEN M & M'S
- LIGHT GREEN MINT M & M'S

## INSTRUCTIONS

IF POPCORN IS DIVIDED INTO VARIETY BAGS, REMOVE ALL BAGS

LINE TIN CAN WITH PARCHMENT PAPER

MELT ALMOND BARK (WHITE) OVER SAUCE PAN OF BOILING WATER IN PARTS,

COMBINE POCORN, SLOWLY DRIZZLED WITH ALMOND BARK, AND CANDIES MIX AND ENJOY!

# *Thoughts*

### Candied Popcorn

A delicious sweet snack that is perfect for movie nights, parties, or just as a special treat. It is made by coating freshly popped popcorn in a sugary syrup, which hardens as it cools to create a crunchy, candy-like coating. There are many different flavors of candied popcorn to choose from, including classic caramel, chocolate, and even fruity flavors like strawberry or blueberry. Candied popcorn is easy to make at home, and can be customized to suit your taste preferences. So why not try making some candied popcorn today and enjoy a tasty and fun snack that the whole family will love!

# WHITE CHOCOLATE & PEPPERMINT DIPPED PRETZELS
## FOOD

Gwendolyn Jones

# Recipe

**INGREDIENTS**
GARLIC CLOVES (MINCED) FRESH EARS OF CORN (DESIRED AMOUNT) BABY RED OR GOLD POTATOES WHITE OR YELLOW ONIONS (TO YOUR PREFERENCE) RED, GREEN AND YELLOW BELL PEPPERS SHRIMP CAJUN AUDOILLE SAUSAUGE TONY'S CREOLE SEASONING OLD BAY SEASONING GARLIC POWDER BLACK PEPPER CRUSHED RED PEPPER FLAKES BUTTER

AFTER CLEANING PREHEAT OVEN 375 DEGREES SLICE/CHUNK BELL PPPERS AND POTATOES (ADD TO LARGE BOWL) SHUCK EARS OF CORN (YOUR DESIRED PREFERENCE) CUT THEM INTO 1 1/2 IN SLICES AND ADD TO BOWL SLICE OR CHUNK ONIONS AND ADD TO BOWL SLICE SAUSAGE AND ADD TO BOWL RINSE SHRIMP (ADD TO BOWL) ADD MINCED GARLIC, DRIZZLE WITH OLIVE OIL OR OIL OF YOUR LIKING AND TOSS ADD SEASONINGS AND TOSS AGAIN FOR EXTRA KICK ADD CRUSHED RED PEPPER FLAKES TAKE ALUMINUM FOIL SHEETS (LAID OUT SEPERATELY) AND SCOOP DESIRED AMOUNT ONTO SHEET WITH A PAT OR TWO OF BUTTER ON TOP. SEAL FOIL AND PLACE ON BAKING SHEET IN OVEN THATS BEEN PREHEATED ON 375 DEGREES 45-1HOUR (APPROXIMATELY)

# thoughts

Covered pretzels are a versatile and delicious snack that offers a sweet and salty flavor. They can be enjoyed at any time of the day, making them a great option for parties, on-the-go, or as a sweet treat after a meal. With a variety of flavors available, including traditional milk chocolate and unique options like white chocolate and peppermint, there is a covered pretzel for everyone. They are also easy to make at home by melting your favorite chocolate and dipping the pretzels in the mixture.

# MIXED BERRY PARFAIT

# Recipe

**INGREDIENTS**
1 BOX WILD STRAWBERRY GELATIN
1 C. EACH STRAWBERRIES
2 C. PREPARED VANILLA PUDDING

1. STEP 1 CAN BE MADE THROUGH STEP 4 UP TO 2 DAYS AHEAD.
2. STEP 2 YOU'LL NEED FIVE 10-OZ GLASS OR PLASTIC GLASSES.
3. STEP 3 PREPARE GELATIN IN A 2-CUP GLASS MEASURE AS BOX DIRECTS. REFRIGERATE, OCCASIONALLY STIRRING GENTLY (TRY NOT TO CREATE BUBBLES), 30 MINUTES OR UNTIL CONSISTENCY OF EGG WHITES.
4. STEP 4 MEANWHILE, STEM AND HULL 1/2 CUP STRAWBERRIES; CUT IN SMALL PIECES COMBINE WITH 1/2 CUP EACH BLUEBERRIES AND RASPBERRIES. DIVIDE FRUIT MIXTURE AMONG GLASSES.
5. STEP 5 ADD GELATIN AND GENTLY STIR WITH A SKEWER TO INCORPORATE BERRIES SO SOME ARE SUSPENDED IN THE GELATIN (DON'T OVERSTIR). REFRIGERATE 3 HOURS OR UNTIL SET.
6. STEP 6 SPOON PUDDING ON GELATIN. STEM, HULL AND SLICE REMAINING STRAWBERRIES AND MIX IN A BOWL WITH REMAINING BLUEBERRIES AND RASPBERRIES; SPOON OVER PUDDING.

# *thoughts*

The Parfait: A Versatile Dish With a Rich History

Originally from France, a parfait is a simple dessert made with cream, eggs, sugar, and syrup. However, in the United States, it has become increasingly popular as a healthy breakfast dish. Consisting of yogurt, granola, and fruit, it's perfect for those busy mornings when you need an extra boost of energy to kickstart your day. Whether you're in the mood for an elegant no-bake dessert or a quick breakfast fix, the parfait is the perfect solution.

# Cheesecake Squares

Try these peanut butter and jam cheesecake squares

# Recipe

INGREDIENTS:

- 100G BUTTER
- 250G DIGESTIVE BISCUITS, CRUSHED INTO FINE CRUMBS
- 500G FULL-FAT SOFT CHEESE
- 100G ICING SUGAR
- 237G CRUNCHY PEANUT BUTTER
- 1 TSP VANILLA EXTRACT
- 300ML DOUBLE CREAM

TOPPING:

- 4 CUBES RASPBERRY JELLY, CHOPPED INTO SMALLER CHUNKS
- 200G FROZEN RASPBERRIES, DEFROSTED
- 1 TBSP CASTER SUGAR

START BY LINING AN 18-20CM SQUARE BAKING TIN WITH BAKING PARCHMENT, ALLOWING THE ENDS TO OVERHANG. THIS WILL MAKE IT EASIER TO REMOVE THE CHEESECAKE LATER. PUT THE BUTTER INTO A LARGE HEATPROOF BOWL THAT HAS A WIDE LIP, AND PLACE IT OVER A SMALLER HEATPROOF BOWL THAT IS FILLED WITH BOILING WATER FROM THE KETTLE. LET IT SIT FOR A MINUTE, THEN STIR UNTIL IT'S COMPLETELY SMOOTH. MIX IN THE CRUSHED BISCUITS, THEN SPOON THE MIXTURE INTO THE PREPARED TIN, PRESSING IT DOWN WITH THE BACK OF A SPOON.

IN A SEPARATE BOWL, BEAT THE SOFT CHEESE, ICING SUGAR, PEANUT BUTTER, AND VANILLA UNTIL WELL COMBINED. IN ANOTHER BOWL, WHISK THE DOUBLE CREAM UNTIL IT JUST HOLDS ITS SHAPE. GENTLY FOLD THIS INTO THE PEANUT BUTTER MIXTURE, THEN SPREAD IT OVER THE BISCUIT BASE AND SMOOTH THE SURFACE WITH A SPOON. CHILL FOR AT LEAST AN HOUR TO SET. IT CAN BE KEPT CHILLED FOR UP TO ONE DAY.

IN THE MEANTIME, POUR THE JELLY CUBES INTO A HEATPROOF BOWL AND ADD 100ML BOILING WATER. STIR TO DISSOLVE, THEN ADD RASPBERRIES AND SUGAR AND CRUSH THE BERRIES WITH A SPOON WHILE STIRRING. POUR THE MIXTURE THROUGH A SIEVE INTO A JUG, THEN POUR IT OVER THE SET CHEESECAKE. CHILL FOR AT LEAST 4 HOURS. IT IS GOOD FOR UP TO TWO DAYS. RUN A KNIFE AROUND THE SIDES AND USE THE OVERHANGING PARCHMENT TO LIFT THE CHEESECAKE ONTO A BOARD. CUT INTO SQUARES.

# Thoughts

Try these peanut butter and jam cheesecake squares. I've chosen a fruit topping, but you could opt for chocolate – turning it into a giant peanut butter cup.

These peanut butter and jam cheesecake squares are a perfect dessert for any occasion. With a creamy peanut butter filling, a layer of sweet strawberry jam, and a crunchy graham cracker crust, these squares are sure to be a hit with everyone. The best part is that they are incredibly easy to make, requiring only a handful of ingredients and minimal effort. If you're feeling adventurous, you can even switch up the toppings and try a chocolate ganache or caramel sauce instead. No matter how you choose to make them, these peanut butter and jam cheesecake squares are sure to satisfy your sweet tooth cravings!

# 06

## PASTA, RICE AND GRAINS

Grain products like bread, cereal, rice, and pasta are good for you. They are important sources of vitamins and minerals. Breads, cereals, rice, and pasta are also good sources of carbohydrates like starch and fiber.

Many people think that starchy foods like breads, rice and pasta are fattening. They are not. But when you add fats like margarine, oil, mayonnaise, cheese sauce or gravy to them, you add many extra calories. Whole-grain foods have more fiber than white grain foods.

There are many kinds of whole-grain foods, such as oatmeal, brown rice, grits, corn tortillas and whole wheat bread. You may want to try a whole grain bread instead of white bread. Use brown rice instead of white rice or mix them together the next time you have rice.

*Nibble Directory*

Some breads and cereals have lots of fat and sugar added when they are manufactured. Croissants, danish, doughnuts, cake and some muffins have more fat and calories than servings of plain breads and cereals. If you enjoy sweet breads and cereals, you don't have to give them up.

Try eating these foods less often or in small amounts. When you shop, read the food labels and look for breads, cereals, rice and pasta mixes that have less fat and sugar in them. You can also cut down on fat when you make rice or pasta dishes.

Try using less oil, butter, or margarine than the recipe says. Sometimes you can cut the fat in half without changing the way the food tastes or looks!

*Nibble Directory*

# Pasta
## sausage, broccoli and Cheese

MESSY CHEF 24

# Recipe

If you're looking for a hearty and delicious meal, try making pasta with sausage and broccoli. Here are the ingredients you will need:

- 1 pound of pasta (penne or fusilli work well)
- 1 pound of Italian sausage (sweet or spicy, depending on your preference)
- 1 head of broccoli, chopped into small florets
- 3 cloves of garlic, minced
- 1/2 cup of chicken broth
- 1/2 cup of heavy cream
- Salt and pepper to taste
- Grated Parmesan cheese for serving

To start, cook the pasta according to the package instructions until it is al dente. While the pasta is cooking, remove the sausage from its casing and brown it in a large skillet over medium heat. Once the sausage is browned, remove it from the skillet and set it aside.

In the same skillet, add the broccoli florets and garlic. Cook for a few minutes until the broccoli is tender and the garlic is fragrant. Add the chicken broth and bring to a simmer. Let the broth reduce by about half, then add the heavy cream and stir to combine.

Add the cooked pasta and sausage back into the skillet with the broccoli and sauce. Toss everything together until the pasta is coated in the sauce. Season with salt and pepper to taste.

Serve the pasta hot, with grated Parmesan cheese on top. Enjoy!

# thoughts

If you are a cheese lover, adding cheese to the heavy creme will make a very cheesy pasta base.

To make the cheese pasta, start by cooking the pasta according to package instructions. While the pasta is cooking, heat the heavy cream in a large skillet over medium heat. Once the cream is hot, add in your favorite shredded cheese, stirring until it's melted and fully combined. Once the cheese sauce is ready, drain the pasta and add it to the skillet with the sauce. Toss the pasta in the sauce until it's fully coated, and serve hot. This cheesy pasta dish is perfect for a quick and easy weeknight dinner or a cozy night in with friends and family.

# HOMEMADE TURKEY TETRAZZINI - NO CANNED SOUP

Ingredients for Turkey Tetrazzini:

8 ounces spaghetti noodles
4 tablespoons unsalted butter
8 ounces sliced button mushrooms
2 teaspoons minced garlic
2 teaspoons fresh thyme leaves (or 1/2 teaspoon dried thyme leaves; not ground thyme)
1/3 cup dry sherry or dry white wine, or chicken stock
1/3 cup all-purpose flour
2 cups low-sodium chicken stock
2 cups milk
1/2 cup grated parmesan cheese
1/4 teaspoon salt
1/2 teaspoon black pepper
1/4 teaspoon grated nutmeg
2 cups cooked, cubed turkey

For the Topping
1 cup panko bread crumbs
¼ cup grated parmesan cheese
3 tablespoons unsalted butter melted
½ teaspoon thyme leaves optional

Preheat the oven to 375°F and grease a 9x13 inch baking dish or 4-quart casserole dish.
Cook the spaghetti noodles in salted boiling water for one minute less than the package instructions. Reserve ¼ cup of pasta water. Drain the noodles and set aside.
In a large saucepan, melt 4 tablespoons of butter over medium-high heat. Add the sliced mushrooms and cook until browned and most of the liquid has evaporated.
Add the thyme leaves and garlic (if using) and cook for 1 minute longer.
Sprinkle the mushrooms with flour and cook for 1 minute to get rid of any raw flour taste. Add in the sherry wine (or dry white wine or chicken stock) and cook until the liquid evaporates.
Slowly whisk in the chicken stock. Add in the milk, nutmeg, salt, and pepper, and bring the sauce to a simmer. Simmer for 5 minutes.
Whisk in the Parmesan cheese and turn off the heat.
Add the cooked turkey and noodles to the cream sauce and stir to combine. If the mixture seems too thick, add in the reserved pasta water.
Pour the turkey and pasta mixture into the prepared casserole dish.
In a separate bowl, mix together the bread crumbs, Parmesan cheese, melted butter, and thyme leaves. Sprinkle the mixture evenly over the turkey casserole.
Bake the turkey tetrazzini until bubbly and golden, for 20-25 minutes.

# thoughts

Tips for making Turkey Tetrazzini include using leftover chicken or turkey, choosing from various noodles, using dry sherry, using panko bread crumbs, and avoiding ground thyme. Leftovers can be stored in an airtight container in the refrigerator for up to four days. The recipe can also be modified by excluding mushrooms or adding up to one cup of mixed vegetables or peas.

# Lasagna
26

Ingredients for a Delicious Lasagna Recipe
Follow this recipe to create a delicious lasagna dish. Here are the ingredients you'll need:

# Recipe

1 kg Beef mince
Produce

1 medium Carrot
1 rib stick Celery
2 Garlic cloves
1 Onion (yellow or brown white)
1/2 tsp each of dried Thyme and Oregano
1 Basil or parsley
2 Bay leaves (dried or fresh)
800 g Tomato
Canned Goods

3 Beef bouillon cubes
1/4 cup Tomato paste
Condiments

2 tsp Worcestershire sauce
Pasta & Grains

350 g Fresh Lasagna
Baking & Spices

1/2 cup Flour
1 Pinch freshly ground Nutmeg
1/2 tsp Salt and Black pepper
1 tsp Sugar
Oils & Vinegars

1 tbsp Olive oil
Dairy

60 g Butter
2 cups Cheese
1 1/2 cups Mozzarella cheese
Beer, Wine & Liquor

1 cup Red wine
Other

4 cups (1 litre) low-fat milk

And here's how you layer it up:

- Smear a bit of meat sauce on the base first – stops the lasagna sheets from sliding around;
- Layer 1 – top with meat sauce, bit of white sauce
- Layer 2 – lay out more lasagna sheets, then top with more meat sauce and more white sauce
- Layer 3 – repeat again, lasagna sheets, meat sauce then white sauce; and
- Topping – cover with lasagna sheets, pour over remaining white sauce then sprinkle with cheese.

# *Thoughts*

The Love for Lasagna: A Worldwide Favorite

Lasagna, oh lasagna! It's no surprise that it's one of the world's most beloved foods. This dish has a way of warming the heart and soul with its comforting and sentimental qualities.

MY SON YA'MAR MAKING HIS PERSONAL PIZZA

# Homemade Pizza

# Recipe

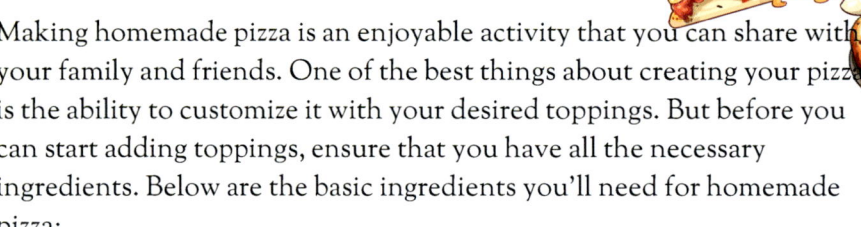

Making homemade pizza is an enjoyable activity that you can share with your family and friends. One of the best things about creating your pizza is the ability to customize it with your desired toppings. But before you can start adding toppings, ensure that you have all the necessary ingredients. Below are the basic ingredients you'll need for homemade pizza:

1. Pizza dough: Flour, yeast, salt and water are the ingredients you need to make your pizza dough. Alternatively, you can purchase pre-made pizza dough from the store.
2. Tomato sauce: A good tomato sauce is essential for any pizza. You can create your sauce using canned tomatoes, garlic, and herbs, or you can buy pre-made pizza sauce.
3. Cheese: Mozzarella cheese is the most commonly used cheese for pizza, but other types like cheddar, parmesan or feta can also be used.
4. Toppings: This is where you can get creative. You can add your preferred toppings like pepperoni, sausage, mushrooms, onions, peppers, olives or pineapple.
5. Flour: Flour is essential for dusting your work surface and preventing the pizza dough from sticking.
6. Cornmeal: To prevent the pizza from sticking to the pizza stone or baking sheet, sprinkle some cornmeal on the surface before placing the dough on it.

By using these basic ingredients, you can create a delicious homemade pizza that's sure to impress your guests. So roll up your sleeves and get ready to knead some dough!

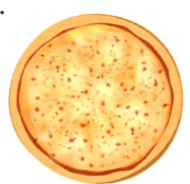

## Thoughts

Making pizza from scratch is a fun way to spend time with loved ones, customize toppings, and experiment with flavors. It's also cost-effective. With simple ingredients like flour, yeast, tomato sauce, cheese, and toppings, anyone can create a delicious pizza, whether it's a classic Margherita or a creative BBQ chicken.

# 07
CAKES AND BAKES

INCORPORATING A SMALL DESSERT INTO YOUR DAILY DIET CAN BE A HEALTHY CHOICE, AS LONG AS YOU MANAGE YOUR PORTION SIZES. KEEP IN MIND, HOWEVER, THAT IT IS CRUCIAL TO MONITOR THE AMOUNT OF SUGAR YOU CONSUME THROUGHOUT THE DAY. ADDED SUGARS CAN BE FOUND IN MANY FOODS, INCLUDING CEREALS, PROTEIN BARS, JUICES, AND BOTTLED TEAS OR COFFEES, SO IT'S ESSENTIAL TO BE MINDFUL OF YOUR DAILY SUGAR INTAKE.

# HOMEMADE PEACH COBBLER

**SHARRON MARSHALL & DR. APRIL A. JONES**

# Recipe

If you're looking for a delicious dessert recipe that will satisfy your sweet tooth, then peach cobbler might be just what you need. Here are the ingredients and recipe you'll need to make this classic dish.

Ingredients:

- 6-7 fresh peaches, peeled and sliced
- 1/2 cup unsalted butter
- 1 cup all-purpose flour
- 1 cup white sugar
- 1 cup milk
- 2 teaspoons baking powder
- 1/2 teaspoon salt
- 1 teaspoon vanilla extract

Instructions:

1. Preheat your oven to 350 degrees Fahrenheit.
2. Melt the butter and pour it into a 9x13 inch baking dish.
3. In a separate bowl, mix together the flour, sugar, baking powder, and salt.
4. Slowly stir in the milk and vanilla extract until the batter is smooth.
5. Pour the batter over the melted butter in the baking dish.
6. Add the sliced peaches on top of the batter.
7. Bake in the preheated oven for 45-50 minutes, or until the top is golden brown and a toothpick inserted in the center comes out clean.
8. Serve the peach cobbler warm with a scoop of vanilla ice cream on top for an extra delicious treat.

Enjoy your peach cobbler!

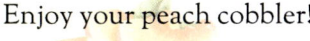

# thoughts

Get ready for a taste explosion! Peach cobbler made from scratch is like a sweet symphony of flavors that'll have you humming all day. This Southern classic is a peachy dream baked into a buttery crust, with a crumbly topping that'll make your taste buds do a happy dance.

Start by slicing up some ripe peaches, then mix them up with sugar, flour, and cinnamon in a bowl. While you let that soak up all the yumminess, get down to business with the crust.

In a mixing bowl, combine flour, sugar, baking powder, salt, and cold butter until it's all crumbly and delicious. Add milk and stir like crazy until it all comes together.

Roll out the crust on a floured surface and pop it into a baking dish. Pour that peachy goodness on top of the crust, and spread it out evenly. Now, for the pièce de résistance: the streusel topping. Combine flour, sugar, and butter in a bowl until it's all crumbly and heavenly. Sprinkle that magic on top of the peaches.

Into the oven it goes, until the crust is golden brown and the peaches are bubbling with delight. Serve it piping hot with a scoop of vanilla ice cream, and let the homemade goodness take over!

# Pancakes

Eating a diet rich in fruits, vegetables, whole grains, and lean protein can have a positive impact on your mental health.

## Recipe

**INGREDIENTS:** 1 CUP ALL-PURPOSE FLOUR 2 TABLESPOONS SUGAR 2 TEASPOONS BAKING POWDER 1/2 TEASPOON SALT 1 CUP MILK 1 EGG 2 TABLESPOONS BUTTER, MELTED 1 TEASPOON VANILLA EXTRACT

**INSTRUCTIONS:** IN A LARGE BOWL, WHISK TOGETHER THE FLOUR, SUGAR, BAKING POWDER, AND SALT. IN A SEPARATE BOWL, WHISK TOGETHER THE MILK, EGG, MELTED BUTTER, AND VANILLA EXTRACT (IF USING). POUR THE WET INGREDIENTS INTO THE DRY INGREDIENTS AND STIR UNTIL JUST COMBINED. DO NOT OVERMIX THE BATTER. HEAT A NON-STICK PAN OR GRIDDLE OVER MEDIUM HEAT. SCOOP 1/4 CUP OF BATTER ONTO THE PAN FOR EACH PANCAKE. COOK UNTIL BUBBLES FORM ON THE SURFACE OF THE PANCAKE AND THE EDGES START TO DRY OUT, THEN FLIP AND COOK FOR ANOTHER 1-2 MINUTES UNTIL GOLDEN BROWN ON BOTH SIDES. REPEAT WITH THE REMAINING BATTER.

SERVE THE PANCAKES WARM WITH YOUR FAVORITE TOPPINGS, SUCH AS MAPLE SYRUP, BUTTER, FRESH FRUIT, OR WHIPPED CREAM. ENJOY!

# thoughts

Who doesn't love pancakes? With their fluffy texture and delicious taste, they are the perfect comfort food. Pancakes are not just for breakfast, but can be enjoyed anytime of the day. Whether you like them with syrup, butter, fruit, or even chocolate chips, pancakes are a versatile treat that can be customized to fit your taste buds. They are also quick and easy to make, making them the perfect go-to meal when you are short on time. So why not indulge in some delicious pancakes today, no matter what time it is?

DR. APRIL A. JONES & SHARRON MARSHALL & KANISHA SIZEMORE

# Brownies with Caramel and Hershey's Chocolate

 # Recipe

Bake Perfect Brownies from Scratch with These Easy Steps

If you're looking for a fun and delicious way to spend an afternoon, try making brownies from scratch. With a few simple ingredients, you can whip up a rich, chocolatey dessert that will satisfy any sweet tooth.

First, gather your ingredients: flour, sugar, cocoa powder, eggs, butter, vanilla extract, and baking powder. Preheat your oven to 350 degrees Fahrenheit and grease a baking dish with cooking spray.

In a large mixing bowl, combine the flour, sugar, cocoa powder, and baking powder. Mix these dry ingredients together until they are well combined. In a separate bowl, whisk together the eggs, melted butter, and vanilla extract.

Add the wet ingredients to the dry ingredients and stir until everything is well mixed. Be careful not to overmix the batter, as this can make your brownies tough.

Pour the batter into your prepared baking dish and use a spatula to smooth it out. Bake in the preheated oven for 20-25 minutes, or until a toothpick inserted into the center comes out clean.

Once your brownies are done, let them cool for a few minutes before slicing and serving. You can enjoy them while still warm with a scoop of vanilla ice cream, or let them cool completely and take them on the go for a sweet treat.

CONTAINS NUTS

## *thoughts*

Get ready to embark on a tasty adventure and craft some scrumptious brownies from scratch! For a real treat, add in some crunchy nuts, chocolate chips, or even a dollop of peanut butter. Get ready to rock and roll in brownie heaven!

"Why splurge on a chef when you've got mini culinary geniuses under your own roof?"

Dr. April A. Jones

www.ingramcontent.com/pod-product-compliance
Lightning Source LLC
Chambersburg PA
CBRC090901080526
44587CB00008B/162